Healing Waters Floating Lamps

Poems by

Kiriti Sengupta

Foreword: Don Martin

Photographs by

Arindam Chowdhury & Somnath Chatterjee

Moments Publication

Published by:
Moments Publication,
4, Suravali Apartment, 33, Jain Nagar,
Paldi, Ahmedabad 380007. [India]

Cover Design: Marut Kashyap
Photographers' Home: http://www.twinlens.in
Typeset by Nikhil Mahajan at Georgia in 11 pts.
ISBN-13: 9789384180232

1st edition [Paperback]: March 27th, 2015
Price: One hundred and fifty rupees only [INR 150/-]

US Dollars: $8.99

Dedicated to the great poet...

The Legendary...

The Unputdownable...

Rabindranath Tagore

In thoughtful contemplation and reflection...

One thing I always enjoy, as I await a new book by Dr. Kiriti Sengupta, is the anticipation. Kiriti is a poet with a broad range, and he writes at ease about topics as diverse as spirituality, family, love and friendship, rural life, native traditions, hobbies, nature, humor, and even some occasional very soft erotica. He also has a formidable arsenal of stylistic tools at his disposal, and he is comfortable with everything from traditionally-structured poetry, to very nearly Japanese-style Haiku, to lyrical, almost song-like work, and even some prose-poetry. The pleasure of the anticipation is that I'm never really sure what I'm going to get! I will say, though, that Dr. Sengupta has never let me down yet!

Healing Waters Floating Lamps is no exception. There's a little something for everyone here, if you'll only take the time to look for it. This is Kiriti's short-form work, and you will find no long epic poems here. That is not to say, however, that these are simple poems without deeper meanings, textures, and nuances. Quite the contrary! This is some complex work, which invites the reader to explore and derive the meanings which seem most suitable to the individual. And in fact I've found, reading some of these poems several times, that what I draw out of them can be different each time, sometimes even depending on my mood! *Fish-Lip* is such a poem for me. I've read it a number of times, and I'm still not sure I know what it means. Or maybe I should say the apparent meaning, to me, changes on rereading and reconsideration. This type of self-directed exploration is what I really love about good, quality, poetry, in the hands of a poet who is a master at handling his images.

Another thing that strikes me about the poems here is they are what I would call "ordinary observations." In much of the modern poetry I read the poet seems to go out of his way to construct arbitrarily complex settings, relationships, fantasies, convolutions, and obfuscations which the reader then has to (sometimes painfully) dissect to extract the essential core nature of the poem. Kiriti has a real knack of describing just the sorts of things we all encounter in our everyday lives, in unpretentious language, so we're all familiar with them. But are we really? Here again I'm not so sure there isn't usually something else lurking just beneath the surface. There almost always is, if we spend some time in thoughtful contemplation and reflection. But be careful! There are some multi-layered meanings here, sometimes clothed in paradox and irony, and it can take some time and considered thought to find them. But that's where the fun is, isn't it?

There is even some irony in the title, *Healing Water Floating Lamps*. The title is drawn from Varanasi, where devotees of Lord Shiva place floating lamps (*diyas*) in the Ganges River. The title seems to imply that what we may find in this book is work which is fluidic, gently flowing, bending only as the subtle contours of the linguistic river requires. But as we start to read what we discover instead are short, hard, almost staccato poems which are throwing out images almost as fast as we can take them in. But if you look at the poems again (as you should; these are not poems to be read only once!) I'm sure you'll find that the poems actually flow quite well. Although some may seem quick and abrupt at first read, I'm confident you'll be able to find and appreciate their melodic textures. The poems actually flow quite well within themselves, and amongst one another. This complex style is not an easy thing to accomplish, and reveals a poet of some high skill and talent.

One thing I've always appreciated about Dr. Sengupta's work is he is able to bring elements of Indian culture and spirituality together in such a way as it's accessible to those who might not have much more than a passing familiarity with the topics. In some cases he'll even include a short explanatory note which highlights certain aspects. I did not know, for example, the symbolic relationship between Koi (the fish) and young girls. Once I understood the Bengali relationship, as explained in Kiriti's note, I was able to more fully explore the poem, *Give Me More of Life*, in which that symbolism is a central theme. This type of gentle explanation is quite welcome, although I will note that Kiriti only goes so far. In no way does he ever try to fully explain the poems to the reader. He gives us only the essential background we need, and then he turns us loose to poke around the nooks and crannies on our own!

Perhaps the final irony of *Healing Waters Floating Lamps* is the physical nature of the book itself. This is a small volume; we do not have in our hands here a 700 page tome filled with densely packed poetry. Yet despite its brevity there is a lot more to this book than it may first appear. As I mentioned, the poems included consist of layers upon layers, with subtle shaded meanings which may only appear after a re-read or two (or more!). I would encourage you to take some time, as I did, to explore at your leisure the various stories, observations, and lessons contained inside. I am quite sure you will come to find that this is, in fact, a "heavy" book. Perhaps not in size and heft, but certainly in scope and depth. I am also quite sure you will also find these poems to contain the essential essence of "healing waters and floating lamps."

Don Martin
March, 2015

[Donald Randolph Martin (Don Martin) is a best-selling author and editor who lives in Tucson, Arizona. His first novel, the futuristic Sol, was published late in the year 2012. He also writes the column View From The Streets, about issues homeless people face, for his blog Random Thoughts. Don is also known as a music writer, who specializes in American Folk, and a book reviewer. When he's not writing or editing you'll find him reading, especially politics and history.]

On the ascending shoots

Your fear matures

A few apprehensions as well

Your roots hold it tighter

Desperately deeper

And much deeper rests your God

Introduction

During an informal meeting with one of my reviewers, Gopal Lahiri, an earth scientist and an Indian poet (who writes in English), he urged, "You have included so many poems in your last two important nonfictional memoirs, *My Glass Of Wine*, and *The Reverse Tree*, it is high time you think about an exclusive collection of your poems." This was, in fact, the source of inspiration of the making of *Healing Waters Floating Lamps*. I have included a few poems that were first published in those books along with a few fresh ones.

I consider poetry my existence. It is indeed challenging to successfully present philosophical and spiritual poems to a larger audience. Now it is up to my readers to decide if I have succeeded in my endeavor.

Thank you,

Kiriti Sengupta

March, 2015

Calcutta

Acknowledgements

I take this opportunity to express my heartfelt gratitude to the following people who not only shared their honest remarks, they made the manuscript stronger by offering their suggestions as well.

K Satchidanandan

Eileen Register

Saikat Majumdar

hülya n. yılmaz

Don Martin

Donna J Snyder

Mary Torregrossa

I was not quite happy with the title that was first planned for this book, and it was Eileen who read the entire manuscript and came up with the present one: *Healing Waters Floating Lamps.*

I am thankful to Ranadeb Dasgupta, an award winning Bengali poet from Calcutta, for offering a few edits that he found necessary in order to preserve the Indian flavor in these verses.

My family has been extremely supportive towards my literary endeavors. Let me express my love to Ma, Baba, Bhaswati (my wife), Aishikk (my son), and Prabir Roy, my younger brother.

Hearty thanks to my publisher for appreciating my work and presenting these verses to the readers.

Table of Contents

Beyond The Eyes

I reach the sky

While I draw a circle in the water

Looking at the image

I take a dip

After Bath

I've bathed your feet with the water of the Ganges
Last dip in the late afternoon, and
I paid my first obeisance
While my body was smeared by the earthen mud

I walked down the broken stairs
With a stony heart
One step down, and down again

I cannot learn swimming ... scared even now

I would not offer a homage anymore
As I offered prayers for the last time

O Sun, I remember
I've bathed your feet with the water of the
Ganges...

[Water of the Ganges, otherwise called Ganga-water, is considered extremely pious, and is widely used in all Hindu religious affairs. And again, the Hindus offer homage to the Sun (called *Surya-pranam*), as it is the sole source of all energies.]

Evening Varanasi

Have you seen the floating lamps in the river?

Water here is not the fire-extinguisher, but
The flames ascend through water

Prayers reach the meditating Lord

[Varanasi (otherwise known as Kashi) is considered the spiritual capital of India (and India being the spiritual capital of the world). Lord *Shiva* is worshipped here with full devotion and in the evening the devotees place tiny lamps (*diyas*) in the river Ganges]

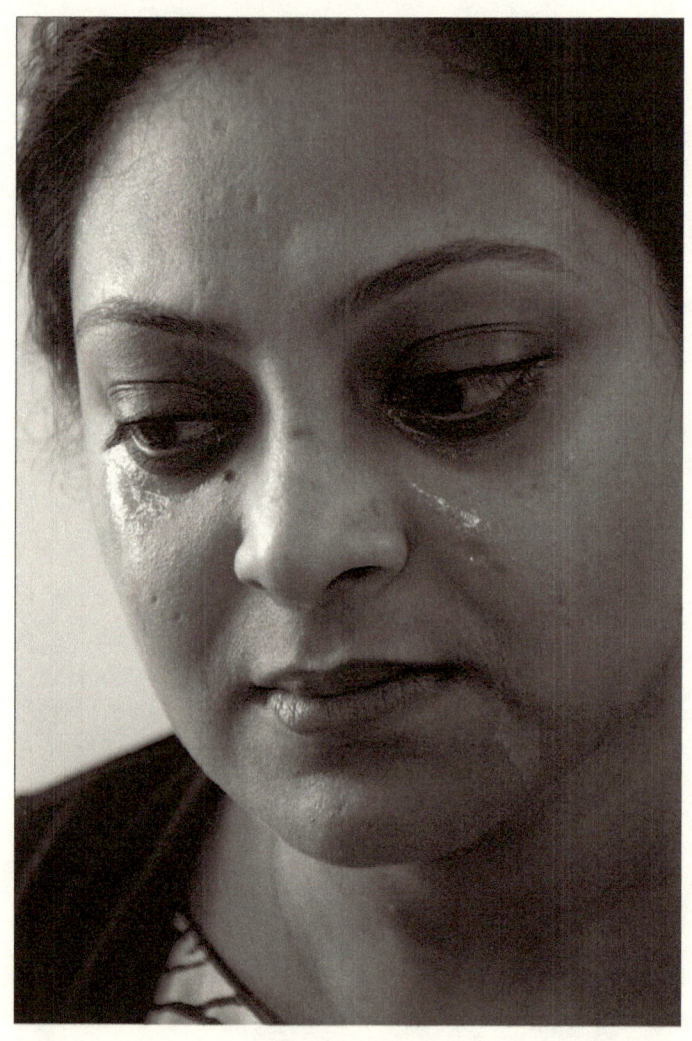

River Of Tears

They have flowed over your eyes
Afraid of being seen
They are shy

In spite of their roomy eyes
They are blind

They don't know
Not all rivers succeed to unite

Unravel

The rear desks are cleaner
And the thriving crowd
Enjoys fast food, lawsuits

Healers worry about the front;
It is dusty, empty, but advocates
Spiritual pursuits

My Master enjoys the stage—
Looking at the sparkling crowd he tells:
"Reach the void, and see the cage"

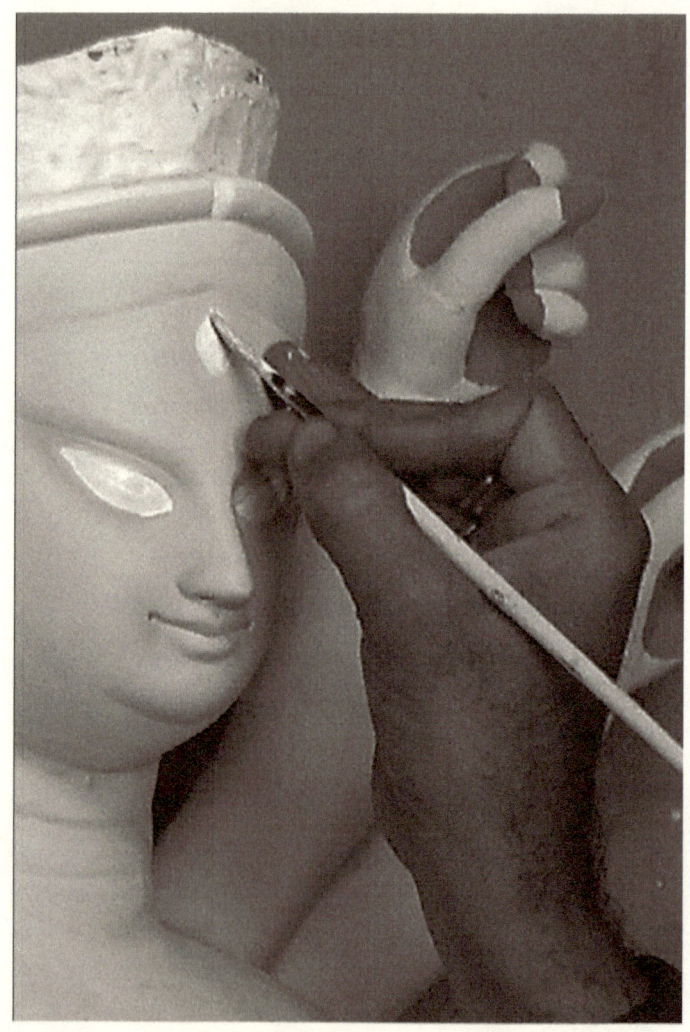

Initiation

My Master made me sit
On the square floor mat, which was brought
In the old bag
I was not facing him at first
My centers were bare
He first touched my base
Gradually coming up
Until he held the cranial recess

He directed me to face him
With my eyes closed
And as soon as he spotted the third eye
My spirit echoed

I fell in love with myself
With the sole existence.

In Dusty Feet

I was about to prostrate,
But refrained from paying an obeisance
To the enlightened Master
His great toes housed
Some holy grains of dust
He took good care of his feet, I guessed,
And I picked the grains as quickly
As to place them on my head

I followed his footsteps,
Even on the dusty roads
I wished to become such pious grains
So as to stay attached with his feet forever

I turned back as I failed,
And could not hold the grains either
On my big toes...

God remained thumb-sized with dusty feet

Eyes Of A Yogi

A mother bird sits on her eggs ... quiet...
Her eyes appear distantly connected to the world

Hey! Look at them
Tiny wings

The mother changes to sky

Communion

The woman in you is sleeping for eons

She wakes up, and

Traverses a lane named serpentine

[An individual carries both a he and a she-energy. The 'she' when awakened traverses the spiral *Kundalini* along the spine and merges with the 'he' that resides at the top of the cranium, commonly referred to as the *Sahasrara*. Upon successful communion an individual turns a Yogi!]

The Enlightened Master

Your teeth never show
As you smile
The world thinks you're tight lipped

You've been flooded with appeals,
And advice to see a speech-therapist,
Or a dentist

Please say, we pleaded...

Did we forget a Yogi seldom breathes?

Color Code

They said you were black
They knew they were white
They loved their eyes

The immigration officers were curious
I pulled my sleeve up to the elbow
Showing them the identifying mark
They grinned...

And I said
This has been the Nelson Mandela *patch*

Clarity

I have seen my mother
Preparing Ghee out of milk—
She never used butter
To clarify it further

She'd boil and store the milk
In large quantities for days
Once cooled, she'd separate
Thick layers of yellow froth—
Layer after layer she filled
The storage pot, then put it on
The burner, which filled
The house with aromatic milk

So organic is my memory—
The granular residue lifted us to heaven
Ah! Pious Ghee, and incorrigible

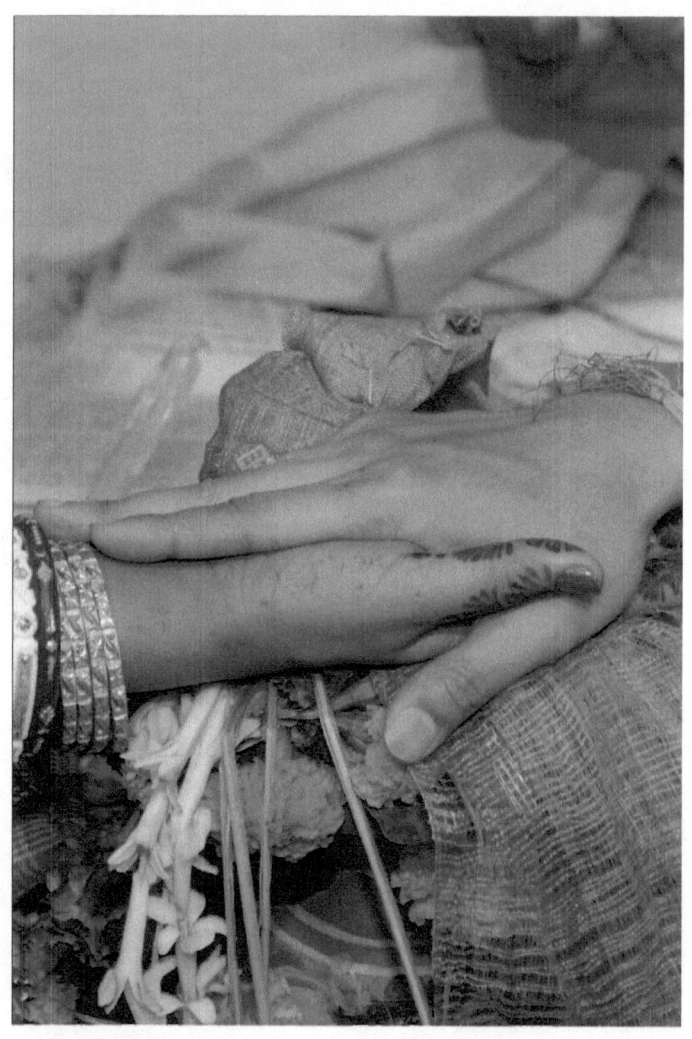

Indian Matrimony

After your sister's wedding her in-laws never failed to pass their comments: "Water and oil don't blend at all..." You could not answer them; they were the respectable elders. You found your sister sweating ... her skin became pale and cold.

You went ahead and explained to them the relationship of economic inflation and the price of crude oil.

You concluded: "Water leaves no mark behind as it evaporates..."

Not in water,
But awake
In the soil

Some poison
Blue...

The venom doesn't fade
Doesn't float
And doesn't even invite!

Touching only a few fingers...

Namesake

1

Whispers the tale of your character
Color and its fragrance merge to call it a rose
A lot matters
If you remember the name...

2

With sheer innocence the boy told the story of his watching movies in a hall named "Nadia Talkies." Sharing the same story for many a time, uttered the name, talkies, and had his face shine! Humble was the hall, so were its viewers. Alas! It is no more ... abolished by the estate promoters! The boy is now a grown up man ... Nadia remains inside its reel-can.

3

The womb carries water — so do your eyes
Water builds the fetus
That becomes 'I'
It's a room for the eyes—
Under the name: 'Rely'

4
Significant indeed — carrying yourself
Crucifixion is Christ-filled!
I remember, and my mind turns candle-lit

They pinned it before,
Will do that now and again...
No arrangements of incense though

God and life
Moving apart

Mellifluous Cry

The labor room was busy as usual

Especially the midwife

*She was visibly unhappy with the silence of the
newborn*

Much worried at it, she patted the back of the baby

The midwife screamed in utter frustration

"Hey! Cry out."

On the other side of the closed door

The father was eager to hear his baby

He was all set to smile and celebrate

The first communication

Secure A River

Hold on, my dear

The word "denser" does not

Necessarily mean thicker

Divine blessings are frequently showered

Unconditionally

The enlightened Masters across the nations

Prefer to name the phenomenon

"Without-A-Cause"

I saw you smiling at your fat donation

Your ailing parents needed you badly

Expecting your assuring presence

You had been calling the payment desk

Every now and then

Only to confirm they had their insurance

Alive

Your parents informed the nurse

A spoonful of water was all they wished

But they departed without you at their bedside

The doctor said your parents didn't struggle

They never complained of your absence

Happy with their pills

They handed over their last will

A piece of paper ... a few words written on it

"When you have time, my child,

Come to the river..."

Memorandum Of Understanding

I'm no linguist!

I know
Air and age are linked
Since eternity

And the wounds surface again
In all directions
Sporting the guise of youth...

Sleep ... Yet To Arrive

As my eyes open wide
I find myself sleeping with half-closed sight
You have come, isn't this right?

You know, I didn't sleep well
For many nights ... many nights

I could hold you
While no candles lit
Only my oil and the vermillion thread
Were among the burning kit

You entered deep into me as did sleep

The moon shone bright
In your seminal light
For many nights ... for many nights

Celluloid

Gold is precious and so is the time
We spent together ... right from the morning tea
Spanning over the lavish lunch until you said,
"Signing off for today."

I was hesitant, you know,
I never said goodbye

Signs are private, and I keep my eyes open
Round the clock

Fish-Lip

I've read morphology of the fish-lip
Gives hint of the water color deep

A small aquarium inside my living room ...
cornered—

Marks of love and kisses

On either side

Even on its face

My lips are thin

No trace of color, but water...

Scratches Are Only Human

Few beautiful scratches, deep within,
Soft marks, palpable even after months—
No wounds, but tiny scratches brown
Soothing, mesmerizing in between!

Lips uncut ... colored, covered are these
Fine lines ... sheer wonder
Scratches see, smile, and talk
Like the palpating vessels that carry
Air straight into my balloons

They smile divine, and growth enhancing—
Climb the crown with shattered reflections,
Moving fingers around, capture my oozing spine...

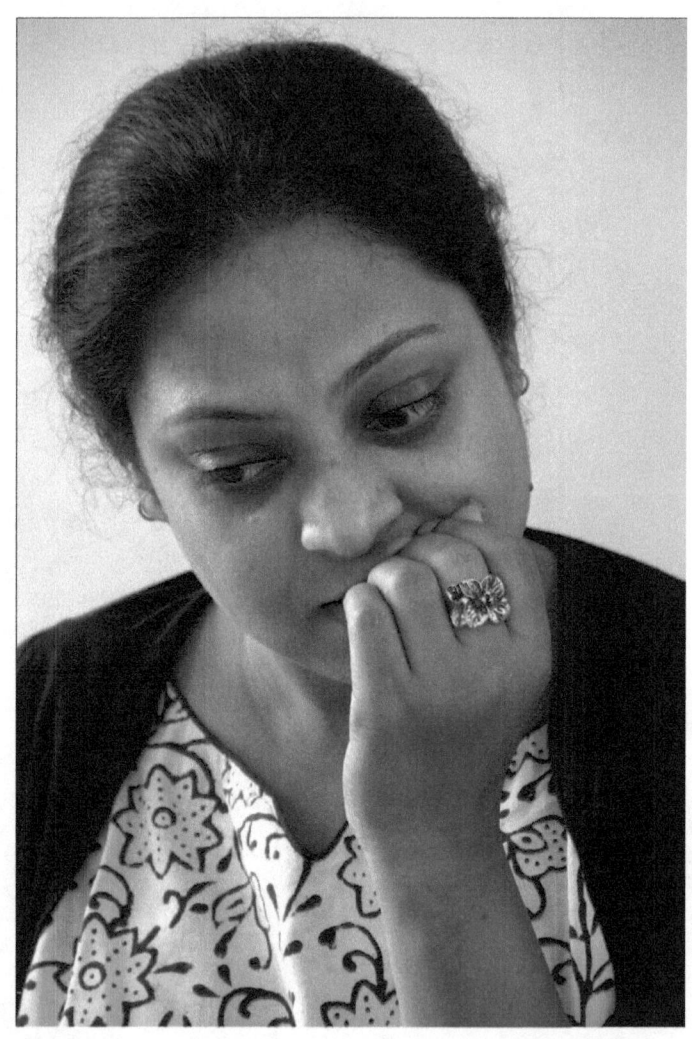

The Odd Number

The night burns
With why, and whys
Those inquiries in a row
End with the mark of a sigh

Scratches made by the nails
Unknowingly
Teeth bite the lower lip

Nauseating smell
Spreads from the damp blanket

Solitary in thy conjugal camp...

The Sun

This is not all about
Day-light photography

This is rather reaching you
As if you're the destination...

Close Circuit

Had not this been fragile
I would have positioned
A camera upon my collar-bone
On either side

And then
I would have removed the extra lenses
One by one...

Ah! Such impeccable folds of civilization

The Morgue

*None has claimed the body yet ... it won't speak on
its own ... to announce identity ... distended with
an unborn life, it seems ... the cover falls short ...
and the limbs remain exposed...*

*Those feet can't take them to the church ... fingers
can no longer light candles...*

*Wish I could burn incense inside the dead room ...
inviting lives ... turning the body into a temple...*

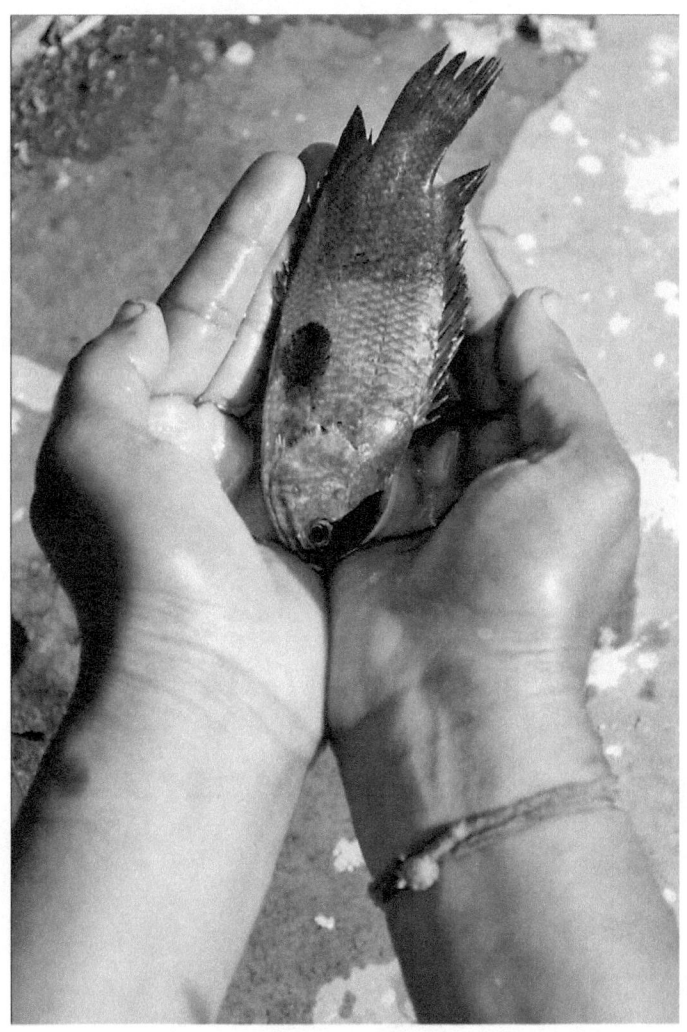

Give Me More Of Life

Amusing, but real...

A young girl was standing
At the bank of a river
Her hands held a live Koi
I was curious, and she said,
"Hold it and you will understand."
She ran away flashing a quick smile

I surfed through the radio channels
On my cell-phone
I heard a commentary of The Gita
A speech on the Visvarupa Darshan

The cellphone blinked
I saw a message my friend sent
A famous line by Tagore—

"Chokher aaloy dekhechilem chokher bahire"

(I envisioned the external through the light of my eyes)

[*Koi* is a fish that survives for a few hours if kept out of water. In Bengali a girl's life is colloquially referred to as a *Koi*'s life, for they can withstand all the hazards that they face.]

Adios

The mirror has a limited role as we urge,
"Please, visit us again."

Immersion happens only in the water
People gather ... they sing and dance
Only a few of them have their eyes moistened

Rituals of self-reflection end
With gods and goddesses
The river turns pregnant

Since Time Unknown

I have not reached yet
The science of you ... I know
I'm glued to, and stand still
With some fixations
Since time unknown
You spin ... continue to swivel
You have a firm grip

Faulty are my limbs
They tilt even on the steady floor
I readily realize
It is all in my mind
As the sky swings

You spin and continue to swirl
Since periods unknown

About the Poet

Dr. Kiriti Sengupta is a bilingual poet and translator in both Bengali and English. He is the author of the bestselling titles, *My Glass Of Wine*, a novelette based on autobiographic poetry, and *The Reverse Tree*, a nonfictional memoir. Kiriti's other works include: *Healing Waters Floating Lamps* [forthcoming; poetry], *My Dazzling Bards* [literary critique], *The Reciting Pens* [interviews of three published Bengali poets along with translations of a few of their poems], *The Unheard I* [literary nonfiction], *Desirous Water* [poems by Sumita Nandy, contributed as the translator], and *Poem Continuous – Reincarnated Expressions* [poems by Bibhas Roy Chowdhury, contributed as the translator]. Reviews of his works can be read on the *Fox Chase Review and Reading Series, Muse India, Red Fez Magazine, Word Riot*, and in *The Hindu Literary Review*, among other places. A few of his books are placed in the Ryerss Museum & Library, Philadelphia, Pennsylvania. Kiriti has also co-edited three anthologies: *Scaling Heights, Jora Sanko – The Joined Bridge*, and *Epitaphs*. He can be reached at http://www.kiritisengupta.com

What People Are Saying

"Delicately poised between a viscerally concrete imagery and a sweepingly abstract philosophy, Kiriti Sengupta's poetry takes us to many places at the same time: the wilted pathways of memory, the teasing tickles of laughter, and when we least expect it, the sharpest splinters of wisdom. Energized by endearing colloquialisms and engaging narratives, this is verse destined for the kind of popular, folkloric life which is the true home of poetry."

> — Saikat Majumdar, the author of two novels, *Silverfish*, and *The Firebird* (forthcoming), and a book of criticism, *Prose of the World*, teaches world literature at Stanford University.

"After a writing record of intensity and versatility, Kiriti Sengupta presents his poetry in English for the first time in *Healing Waters Floating Lamps* . The author's refined sense of command over the intended content displays itself throughout the book, including the patches of the occasional short prose. Whether he seeks depth through brevity in seemingly common-day-symbolism or surprises with sensual imagery to a subtle invite to imagination, his written word reaches out to his audience with impact. The melodic tune of *Sleep ... Yet to Arrive* then takes the reader to a yearning-filled slumber of love, while *After Bath* leaves them eagerly waiting for ritual in "the water of the Ganges" of which Sengupta tells. With his newest book, in other words, the author sates yet once again the reading appetite of an audience that awaits variety."

— hülya n. yılmaz, Liberal Arts professor, The Pennsylvania State University, U.S.A.; Author of *Trance,* a collection of poems in English, German and Turkish by Inner Child Press, Ltd.

"Sengupta's *Healing Waters Floating Lamps* connotes ethereality in different hues. Water suggests movement, fluidity. The poems are marked by movement, in their short frame, staccato like. They remind one of Tagore's mysticism and colors abound in the poems. At the same time Sengupta is a poet of a lost world, the rural life epitomized here by Nadia. The Bengali synecdoche of the poems is also present — the reference to a woman, likened to a fish ... the Koi fish. These are powerful poems not because of any daredevilry, but because of their interesting blend of tradition and modernity, thought and feeling. This is evident in both style and structure. Form and content are contiguous. The sensory "escapism" if one may call it, a spiritual force, is rooted in the Bengali culture. Always experimenting, Sengupta is poised to break new grounds in English poetry."

> — Ananya S Guha is a Senior Academic, widely published poet, and a well-known critic from Shillong, India.

"In *Healing Waters Floating Lamps*, Sengupta's poetry refuses to be limited, addressing everything from meditation practice to achieve spiritual perfection, Hindu rituals involving the Ganges River, the precarious position of a bride when the family into which she married is hostile, photography, and classical poetry. Most poems make use of very forthright, unpretentious language and appear to express simple observations from the poet's life. Other poems are lyrical, such as "the mother [bird] changes to sky," a line that makes a reader's heart leap up with both delight and recognition."

— Donna J Snyder, a poet from El Paso, Texas, and author of *Poemas ante el Catafalco: Grief and Renewal* and *I Am South*. Recognized for her work as an activist lawyer on behalf of indigenous people, immigrant workers, and people with disabilities.

"Deep poetry, multi-layered meaning ... *Healing Waters Floating Lamps* is not for the casual poetry reader who simply seeks melody, rhyme and rhythm. Kiriti Sengupta writes poems that require in-depth thinking to capture the true essence of his words. At first obscure in some cases, upon further examination, his prose and sensual poetry reveals the deeper, more profound knowledge of life captured within them. To understand them is to begin to know the poet's complex psyche, his emotions, and the very heart of his culture. India is revealed through the heart and eyes of a true poet."

— Eileen Register is an author, teacher, and owner of The International Directory of Published Authors, Florida, U.S.A.